AF228772

Nepal Jungle Safari

by Grace Hansen

abdobooks.com

Published by Abdo Kids, a division of ABDO, P.O. Box 398166, Minneapolis, Minnesota 55439.
Copyright © 2025 by Abdo Consulting Group, Inc. International copyrights reserved in all countries.
No part of this book may be reproduced in any form without written permission from the publisher.
Abdo Kids Jumbo™ is a trademark and logo of Abdo Kids.

Printed in the United States of America, North Mankato, Minnesota.

052024

092024

THIS BOOK CONTAINS
RECYCLED MATERIALS

Photo Credits: Alamy, Getty Images, Shutterstock

Production Contributors: Teddy Borth, Jennie Forsberg, Grace Hansen
Design Contributors: Victoria Bates, Candice Keimig

Library of Congress Control Number: 2023948681
Publisher's Cataloging-in-Publication Data

Names: Hansen, Grace, author.

Title: Nepal jungle safari / by Grace Hansen

Description: Minneapolis, Minnesota : Abdo Kids, 2025 | Series: World safaris | Includes online resources
and index.

Identifiers: ISBN 9798384900849 (lib. bdg.) | ISBN 9798384901549 (ebook) | ISBN 9798384901891
(Read-to-me eBook)

Subjects: LCSH: Safaris--Juvenile literature. | Natural areas--Juvenile literature. | Nepal--Description and
travel--Juvenile literature. | Jungles--Juvenile literature. | Wilderness areas--Juvenile literature. | Travel-
-Juvenile literature.

Classification: DDC 954.96--dc23

Table of Contents

Let's Go on Safari!

Nepal is a country in South Asia. It is home to some of Earth's most unique animals. Let's go on safari in the jungles of Nepal!

Asia
Nepal

A safari is a tour where people can see wild animals in their **habitats**. There are many ways to go on safari in the jungles of Nepal. Some people go by foot or Jeep. Others go by canoe.

Jungle Animals of Nepal

Several hundred bird species live in the jungles of Nepal, including kingfishers. The best way to see them is often by canoe. Kingfishers perch above the river on overhanging branches. They dive for fish.

In the fresh waters below, gharials also hunt for fish. These interesting-looking crocodiles can grow up to 15 feet (4.6 m) long.

On land, Indian rhinoceros graze on grasses. They live in the **foothills** of the Himalayas in grasslands and forests. The best time to spot them is in the early morning hours.

Up the **rugged** Himalayan landscape is one of Nepal's most beautiful animals. The red panda can be found in treetops where it feasts on forest fruits.

Back down in the lowland forests, sloth bears can be found. They use their long tongues and claws to catch and eat insects. There is a good chance of seeing these bears on safari!

A small population of Asian elephants also live in Nepal's forests. They are found near fresh water sources. Females form **herds** of around 7 elephants.

One of the most endangered
species in the world lives in
Nepal. The powerful Bengal tiger
lives alone and avoids humans.
Seeing one would be a highlight
of a Nepal jungle safari!

Nepal Jungle Experiences

Bungee Jump in a Gorge
Kodari

Go White-Water Rafting
Trishuli River

Paraglide off a Cliff
Pokhara

Zipline above the Jungle
Kathmandu

Glossary

endangered – in danger of becoming extinct.

foothill – a lower hill near the base of a mountain or group of mountains.

habitat – the natural environment of a plant or animal.

herd – any group of wild animals that feed and travel together.

perch – to rest or come to rest on a branch.

rugged – having a surface that is rough and broken.

species – a group of living things that look alike and can have young together.

Index

Visit **abdokids.com** to access crafts, games, videos, and more!